In the Holy Quiet of This Hour

A Meditation Manual

Richard S. Gilbert

Skinner House Books
Boston

Published by Skinner House Books,
an imprint of the Unitarian Universalist Association,
25 Beacon Street, Boston, MA 02108-2800.

Printed in Canada.

10 9 8 7 6 5 4 3 2 1
99 98 97 96 95

To my mother, Hazel Gilbert, who points the path
To my wife, Joyce, who walks with me now
To my sons, Matthew and Douglas, who follow

Contents

Preface

The title for this book is from my favorite passage in *Hymns of the Spirit*, our 1937 hymnal published by Beacon Press. "In the holy quiet of this hour" is a phrase that reflects my belief that meditation is a precious moment of calm reflection on the intimacies and ultimacies of human existence. It is a preparation for and a reflection on what poet Wallace Stevens calls "moments of inherent excellence," in which we experience our unity with all that is. The beauty of this phrase is that it speaks to people of all theological persuasions.

These meditations were designed for corporate worship, though several were reflections used in sermons or newsletter columns. They grew out of personal experience, most often encountered in the day-to-day "walking together" of a Unitarian Universalist congregation. They emerged from particular incidents in the life of a single community, growing from the experiential soil of minister and congregation living together.

The theological and liturgical style of these meditations is essentially that of a mystical religious humanist—one who cannot bring himself to formal prayer, but believes he experiences something very much akin to it.

One of my seminary professors said anyone can be original if one is ignorant enough. I have attempted to briefly note sources for quotes, but no doubt have unconsciously borrowed ideas from others. Writing is a great river in which many streams converge.

The natural seasons of the earth, as well as the movement of the liturgical year, are reflected in my moods, and are the glue that holds these meditations together.

I hope this collection will help others find "the holy quiet of this hour" which has sustained me over the years.

An Affirmation

In the love of beauty
and the spirit of truth
we unite
for the celebration of life
and the service of humanity.

At Homeness

Be silent, be still, be serene in this house of the spirit.
Put aside all noises that annoy, all sounds that irritate,
The cacophony that confounds.
Here you are at home.

Leave behind all the frustrations that belittle,
The causes that fret, the troubles that torment.
Here you can be at rest.
Put away all the plans to be made,
Things to be done, victories to be won.
Here you are at peace.

Breathe deeply.
Clear the mind of all cluttered thought.
Purge the spirit of all unkindness.
Rinse the soul clean and pure.
Here you are at home.

Sit easy and be at rest.
Feel your body recover its resilience,
Your mind its bearings, your spirit its strength.
Once again we have come home to the Source.
We feel the collective power of our companions,
The warmth of their welcome, the support of their caring.
We who have been wanderers, groping for something, we
know not what,
Are again at home.
Here is the place for us.

We are at home in this sanctuary
And with these people;
We are at home on this globe
And with all who dwell upon it;
We are at home in this cosmos,
Our home for all times past
And all time to come.

We are at home here.

We Are All More Human Than Otherwise

The human race is a vast rainbow,
white, black, red, yellow, and brown
bursting into view.
Yet for all,
blood is red,
the sky is blue,
the earth brown,
the night dark.

In size and shape we are a varied pattern of
tall and short,
slim and stout,
elegant and plain.
Yet for all there are
fingers to touch,
hearts to break,
eyes to cry,
ears to hear,
mouths to speak.

In tongue we are a tower of babel,
a great jumble of voices grasping for words,
groping for ways to say love, peace, pity, and hope.

Faiths compete, claiming the one way;
saviors abound, pointing to salvation.
Not all can be right, not one.
We are united only by our urge to search.

Boundaries divide us, lines drawn to mark our diversity,
maps charted to separate the human race from itself.
Yet a mother's grief,
a father's love,
a child's happy cry,
a musician's sound,
an artist's stroke,
batter the boundaries and shatter the walls.

Strength and weakness,
arrogance and humility,
confidence and fear
live together in each one,
reminding us that we share a common humanity.
We are all more human than otherwise.

The Chalice of Our Being

"Each morning we must hold out the chalice of our being to receive, to carry, and give back."—Dag Hammarskjold

Each morning we hold out our chalice of being
To be filled with the graces of life that abound—
Air to breathe, food to eat, companions to love,
Beauty to behold, art to cherish, causes to serve.

They come in ritual procession, these gifts of life.
Whether we deserve them we cannot know or say,
For they are poured out for us.
Our task is to hold steady the chalice of our being.

We carry the chalice with us as we go,
Either meandering aimlessly,
Or with destination in our eye.

We share its abundance if we have any sense,
Reminding others as we remind ourselves
Of the contents of the chalice we don't deserve.
Water from living streams fills it
If only we hold it out faithfully.

We give back, if we can, something of ourselves—
Some love, some beauty, some grace, some gift.
We give back in gratitude if we can
Something like what is poured into our chalice of being—
For those who abide with us and will follow.

Each morning we hold out the chalice of our being,
To receive, to carry, to give back.

Wind Chimes at My Window

I sit in my office at work, my mind full of ideas—too many ideas—when suddenly and without warning a gentle breeze moves through the window and stirs my wind chimes. Their gentle ringing distracts me from the buzz of my computer and transports me to another realm. It is sheer beauty, an exquisite sound that resonates with the deep places of my being.

I stand in a monastery courtyard, taken with the beauty of carefully raked gravel, lovely bushes, and bamboo. It is all too perfect—it could not have been arranged any other way. A gong sounds, a deep, mellifluous chime that seems to come from an eternal past and beckons me to contemplation. Its resounding tone reminds me of the mystery within.

I purchase a small bell, a replica of the great gong. It hardly imitates the gong's majesty, but it reminds me that I have an inner life, that everyone has an inner life. It is a reminder to take time for the journey within.

Wind over chimes, hammer on gong, tiny clapper on bell—sounds of the spirit, sounds that have echoed down through the ages, sounds that have inspired monks and priests and priestesses and gurus and oracles and prophets and all who have aspired to hear the inner music of creation, sounds that speak of ultimate things—music for healing the heart.

The breeze blows in my window again and stirs the wind chimes. A tiny tinkling becomes a melodious scale—and I hear for a time an inner music that restores, and I am glad.

Life Is Always Unfinished Business

In the midst of the whirling day,
In the hectic rush to be doing,
In the frantic pace of life,
Pause here for a moment.

Catch your breath;
Relax your body;
Loosen your grip on life.

Consider that our lives are always unfinished business;
Imagine that the picture of our being is never complete;
Allow your life to be a work in progress.

Do not hurry to mold the masterpiece;
Do not rush to finish the picture;
Do not be impatient to complete the drawing.
From beckoning birth to dawning death we are in process,
And always there is more to be done.

Do not let the incompleteness weigh on your spirit;
Do not despair that imperfection marks your every day;
Do not fear that we are still in the making.

Let us instead be grateful that the world is still to be created;
Let us give thanks that we can be more than we are;
Let us celebrate the power of the incomplete;
For life is always unfinished business.

A Tomb Is No Place to Stay

A tomb is no place to stay,
Be it a cave in the Judaean hills
Or the dark cavern of the spirit.

A tomb is no place to stay
When fresh grass rolls away the stone of winter cold
And valiant flowers burst their way to warmth and light.

A tomb is no place to stay
When each morning announces our reprieve,
And we know we are granted yet another day of living.

A tomb is no place to stay
When life laughs a welcome
To hearts that have been away too long.

The Empty Chair

There is something about an empty chair
That reminds us of our ultimate loneliness,
Evoking memories of those we have loved and lost.
No longer will they occupy that chair,
However much their image is etched in our memory.

Chairs know the comings and goings of people,
The assault of young bodies
And the gentler weight of old ones.
They know the passing of the years;
They absorb all in well-worn wood.

There is something in us
That doesn't like an empty chair,
That wants it occupied
By the ones we love and loved.
Its presence haunts us with memories that fade
But do not die.

We reach out across empty space,
Encircling nothing but a memory.
Our fingers caress the well-known cracks and grooves,
As familiar to us as the body that filled them.
Our eyes create the image of a former time
When loved ones brought a chair to life
And endeared it to us.

Now there is little to do but sit,
Supported by the strength of years,
Occupying beloved space for a time,

Rejoicing in times gone by, never to return.
People, like chairs, are full of memories,
Memories that sustain our coming in and our going out
From this day forward.

Celebrate the Interval

Life is a brief interval between birth and death;
It is composed of a few notes between Prelude and Postlude;
It is a drama quickly played between the rising and falling of
    a curtain.

What shall we do with that interval of time?
What combination of notes shall we play?
What thespian mask shall we wear?

The transcience of life tempers our joy;
Discordant notes reverberate in the soul;
The ending of the play is ever in doubt.

Yet the brevity can be rich with joy;
A simple tune caresses our ears;
The play produces laughter from time to time.

Why, then, are we so careless with time?
Why do we not sound the music of our hearts?
Why do we not feel the stage beneath our feet?

Is it not time to enjoy the interval?
Is it not time to play our own melody?
Is it not time for us to act our part?

Life is a brief interval between birth and death.
May we celebrate the interval with joy;
May we sing the song that belongs to us;
May we act as if our very life depended on it.

It does.

Loneliness and Love

Loneliness is our common fate.
There is no escape.
But out of that loneliness comes our salvation,
For we love out of our fear of being alone.
As long as human beings people the earth,
We can be assured
That in our loneliness
There is also love—
Deep, infinite love,
Waiting to be tapped,
To water the barren brown lawn of our loneliness—
Love which shrivels if kept to the self,
Which flourishes only if it is given away.

I need you.
You need me.
I know it.
You know it.
What are we waiting for?

We Are, Therefore, We Love

We are, therefore, we love.
Cosmic bits of mass and energy
Come to life together.
We love, therefore, we are.
May we be humble before the wonder
Of what we dare to create.

The Courage of Patience

When we are overwhelmed with the world
And cannot see our way clear,
When life seems a struggle between tedium and apathy
Or frenzy and exhaustion,
When today seems a punishment and tomorrow a torment,
May we find the courage of patience.

May we recognize courage in ourselves and our companions
That is not dramatic, that elicits no fanfare,
That commands little notice by the world,
That is forgotten and taken for granted.

May we learn how to cope
Like those who live one day of pain at a time,
Who see the long path of suffering and do not despair,
Who inspire us by their patient courage,
When we are impatient and afraid.

May we know such courage
And quietly celebrate its presence among us.

We Meet on Holy Ground

We meet on holy ground,
For that place is holy
Where lives touch, love moves, hope stirs.

How much we need this moment before the eternal,
The time to be in reverence before the ultimate,
The pause that renews,
The interlude that refreshes,
The space that gives us room to be.

We meet on holy ground,
Brought into being as life encounters life,
As personal histories merge into the communal story,
As we take on the pride and pain of our companions,
As separate selves become community.

How desperate is our need for one another:
Our silent beckoning to our neighbors,
Our invitations to share life and death together,
Our welcome into the lives of those we meet,
And their welcome into our own.

May our souls capture this treasured time.
May our spirits celebrate our meeting
In this time and in this space,
For we meet on holy ground.

The Nourishing Dark

We pause in holy quiet of the nourishing dark.

The days are shorter now—darkness overtakes light.
We miss the sparkling daylight hours,
The long days of brightness and activity.
We yearn for their swift return,
And wonder if we can wait,
Or if our patience will at last give out.

We forget the nourishing dark at our peril.
There is mystery in the dark to be probed.
There is the adventure of that which cannot be known,
Cannot be seen—can only be experienced in the soul.
There is deepness in the dark, impenetrable and inviting.

In the darkness we rest our bodies and our souls;
We escape that which distracts and confuses;
We come face to face with ourselves;
We come into the deep places of our being.

Darkness is not mere absence of light.
Darkness is not simply an interval between days.
Darkness is the softness of things,
The blessed quiet of the night.

May we not bemoan the dark, but relish it.
May we feel its powerful presence
And rejoice in its mystical embrace.
May we celebrate the deep and nourishing dark.

Thanks Be for These

For the sound of bow on string,
Of breath over reed,
Of touch on keyboard;

For slants of sunlight through windows,
For shimmering shadows on snow,
For the whisper of wind on my face;

For the smooth skin of an apple,
For the caress of a collar on my neck;

For the prickling of my skin when I am deeply moved,
For the pounding of my heart when I run,
For the peace of soul at day's end;

For familiar voices in family rites,
For the faces of friends in laughter and tears,
For the tender human arms that hold me;

For the flashes of memories that linger,
For the mysterious moments that beckon,
For the particularity of this instant;

For the silence of moon-lit nights,
For the sound of rain on my roof,
Of wind in dry leaves,
Of waves caressing the shore;

For the softness of summer breezes,
For the crispness of autumn air,

For dark shadows on white snow,
For the resurrection of spring,
For the faithful turning of the seasons;

For angular, leafless trees,
For gentle hills rolling in the distance,
For meandering streams seeking an unseen sea;

For cornstalks at stiff attention,
And brittle plants bristling past their prime,
For unharvested gardens returning plants to enrich the
    soil;

For the sight of familiar faces,
The sound of our spoken names,
The welcoming embrace of outstretched arms;
For the ritual of friendship,
Reminding us we matter:
Thanks be for these.

Fancy and Fact

Let us learn to play with life,
For we seem to work too hard at it.
Let us learn to sing when we have only spoken,
For the melody casts our words on winds of hope.
Let us learn to enjoy cadencies of poetry instead of pages of
    prose,
For they may be closer to the rhythms of life.
Let us make room for fancy while we give fact a rest.

Let us take more time to build a snowman than to shovel a
    walk.
Let us lift our face to the heavens
And let the snow caress our eyes and tantalize our tongues,
While we forget its treacheries underfoot.
Let us learn to smile when we are tired with the work we
    have to do.
Let us laugh when our tensions give rise to anger.
Let us learn to be merciful when we want to be judgmental.

Let us play in the fields of myth and legend,
For news and facts will always be there.
Let us sample the whimsical words of the poets
More than the studied words of the scholars.
Let our thoughts roam in realms of imagination
Rather than linger in quagmires of reality.

May hope find its way into our hearts
Even when our minds tell us there is no hope.
May charity speak to us even when we have nothing to give.
May loving kindness be with us when our store of love is
    exhausted.
Let it be so for a time, for a season,
And perhaps that season will linger and take hold,
Never to let us go.

Gentleness in Living

Be gentle with one another—

It is a cry from the lives of people battered
By thoughtless words and brutal deeds;
It comes from the lips of those who speak them,
And the lives of those who do them.

Who of us can look inside another and know what is there
Of hope and hurt, or promise and pain?
Who can know from what far places each has come
Or to what far places each may hope to go?

Our lives are like fragile eggs.
They crack and the substance escapes.
Handle with care!
Handle with exceedingly tender care
For there are human beings within,
Human beings as vulnerable as we are,
Who feel as we feel,
Who hurt as we hurt.

Life is too transient to be cruel with one another;
It is too short for thoughtlessness,
Too brief for hurting.
Life is long enough for caring,
It is lasting enough for sharing,
Precious enough for love.

Be gentle with one another.

Overwhelmed by Being

There are times when we feel overwhelmed by being,
We are on a treadmill walking hurriedly, going nowhere;
The images of our lives fly past us as on a movie screen,
The hands of the clock we see actually moving—too quickly.

At such times we need to gather ourselves together,
Slacken our pace,
Blank out the screen,
Ignore the clock.

Then we can remind ourselves that we are in charge of our
    lives,
That it is we who dictate the pace,
We who can choose to stop the rapidly moving screen,
That we can set the rhythm of our own lives.

It will not be easy—it is never easy to convert ourselves,
To turn ourselves around,
To get some kind of handle on the story of our own lives,
To realize that we are the architects of our own fate.

To be sure, there are powers and principalities that confront
    us;
The demands on our time and energy are endless,
We cannot fully control our environment;
We are, after all, finite and flawed creatures.

But out of that finitude comes a yearning for meaning,
Out of the flawed nature of our being we yearn for purpose,
Out of the hectic rush of events we can still set our own pace.
We are the only ones who can.

On Facing the Inevitable

There is a story of a little girl sent by her mother on an errand. When she finally returned, her mother asked what took her so long. A friend had broken his bicycle and she had stopped to help. "But," her mother said, "you don't know anything about fixing bicycles." "I know," she said. "I stopped to help him cry."

We come here in the presence of the Ultimate Mystery, knowing we are bound by the inevitables of life. Determined as we are to "fix" things, to make all things right, to display our mastery over fate, in our wiser moments we know our limits. Sometimes, all we can do is sit in the presence of one another and cry.

Always are we trying to assert ourselves in the face of life's difficulties. We need to feel that we can overcome them, that we can triumph over adversity. Sometimes, in the face of the imponderable, all we can do is sit with another and love.

We are all too human in our need to feel our superiority to the things of nature. Neither beasts nor flowers of the field are we, rather the crowning glory of creation. We are also creatures who have only begun to explore our limits. Sometimes, in the face of the unchangeable, all we can do is sit with another and laugh.

May we forgive our arrogance, understand our pride, be gentle with our presumptions. It is only that we are human, that our reach exceeds our grasp, that we try so hard to be gods. In the face of the divine, all we can do is stay with one another and be human.

God Is a Three Letter Word

God is . . .
A three letter word,
Partner in profanity,
Companion of the sublime,
The deepest down darkness in me,
The rainbow wrapped around my shoulder,
The mystery beyond all knowing
or wanting to know,
The poet's literary friend,
The justifier of a thousand horrible deeds
and the why of a million-billion acts of love.
The question as inescapable
as it is unanswerable,
The macro-cosmic mystery
and the micro-cosmic explanation,
The word when there is a desert
with nothing to say,
And the subject of a jungle of books.
The without which nothing
and with which what?
God is the theist's joy,
The atheist's foil,
The agnostic's doubt.
God is a simple
     deep
         dark
             light
             bright
up-tight
     three letter word.

In Betweenness

We live
In between festivals of gratitude and joy,
In between seasons of contrasting color,
Between floods of brightness
And seas of whiteness.

We live
On a remote island outpost in fathomless space,
Between stars and moons and planets and void,
Surrounded by meteors, comets, rays, and nothingness
In which there is no right or left, up or down—
Only betweenness.

We live
Not quite at the apex of joy,
Nor in the nether of sorrow,
But in the moving space between,
Uncertain of our location.

We live
Walking from city of birth to death,
Hoping along the way
To see something of beauty,
To touch hands with those we love,
To give more than we get,
To make some sense of it all.
We live in betweenness.

Prayer for the Hurried, the Undisciplined, and the Disorganized

O Spirit that hears prayer, attend to these words:
I would say a prayer for the hurried ones,
Those who are spiritually undisciplined,
Those whose lives are disorganized.

Thou must indeed hear the prayers of the deliberate ones,
Those whose religious discipline is cause for admiration,
Those whose lives are in good order.
Hear my plea for those who are in too much of a hurry;
Help to slow them down to hear the patient word of truth;
Attend my prayer for those who know not how to pray
That they might still partake of sources of strength;
Let me plead for those whose lives are dishevelled,
That they might know the sustaining strength of order.
Help us understand that the still, small voice comes to us,
Not only in the solemn setting of the sanctuary,
But in the hustle and bustle of our lives.
Help us know that sacred stillness sometimes greets us
When we seem least prepared to receive it;
Help us understand that the divine order of things
Supports us even in our confusion.
Let us seek to slow ourselves down;
Let us seek to cultivate disciplines of the spirit;
Let us seek to order our lives into works of beauty.

But, God of hurry and repose, Lord of discipline and impulse,
Spirit of the organized and disorganized,
Accept those of us who will never stop running;
Be patient with those of us who cannot discipline ourselves;
Bless us who never seem to get our lives together.

To Savor the World or Save It

"It's hard to know when to respond to the seductiveness of the world and when to respond to its challenge. If the world were merely seductive, that would be easy. If it were merely challenging, that would be no problem. But I arise in the morning torn between the desire to improve the world and a desire to enjoy the world. This makes it hard to plan the day."

—E. B. White

I rise in the morning torn between the desire
To save the world or to savor it—to serve life or to enjoy it;
To savor the sweet taste of my own joy
Or to share the bitter cup of my neighbor;
To celebrate life with exuberant step
Or to struggle for the life of the heavy laden.
What am I to do when the guilt at my bounty
Clouds the sky of my vision;
When the glow which lights my every day
Illumines the hurting world around me?
To savor the world or save it?
God of justice, if such there be,
Take from me the burden of my question.
Let me praise my plenitude without limit;
Let me cast from my eyes all troubled folk!
No, you will not let me be. You will not stop my ears
To the cries of the hurt and the hungry;
You will not close my eyes to the sight of the afflicted.
What is that you say?
To save, one must serve?
To savor, one must save?

The one will not stand without the other?
Forgive me—in my preoccupation with myself,
In my concern for my own life
I had forgotten.
Forgive me, God of justice,
Forgive me, and make me whole.

In Praise of Doubt

It is not that we are not believers.
It is that our belief
Has to be passed through the fires of skepticism
And boiled in the crucible of doubt.

You have heard it said,
"Ours is not to reason why,
Ours is but to do and die."
But I say unto you,
Ours is not to doubt and die,
Ours is to seek the reason why.

When we doubt, we affirm the importance of reason
And our confidence in ourselves as centers of religious
    authority.
When we doubt, we affirm the seriousness of the religious
    quest.
When we doubt, we recognize that truth was not engraved in
    stone 2,000 years ago.
When we doubt, we acknowledge that our understanding of
    truth is imperfect.
When we doubt, we strengthen our faith.

For the faith of doubt we give thanks;
For the doubt of faith we make glad thanksgiving.
For the courage of adventure
That welcomes questions
As much as answers;
For the beloved community of seekers,
We sing our alleluias into the silent darkness.

A Cry That Splits the Night

The night splits with a wild primordial cry,
And against the moon-gray sky
A faint, victorious band of geese knifes its way north,
Their flight accompanied by a sound
That must shake the earth to its foundation,
And I am roused from my slumber.
It is a cry from the deep bowels of earth;
It is a cry, ancient as the species,
A cry of the turning earth,
A cry of coming warmth and light.
The sound resonates in my silent wintry heart as no other,
For it is a mystic sound that stretches my soul,
Reminding me of elemental forces,
Mysterious instincts of survival
To which I am not party, but an awe-struck observer.
On they sweep across the sky to an unknown destination;
Some watering place will receive them,
Sustain them for a season,
And then that same mysterious inner prompting
Sends them flying once more, leaving me behind,
Witness to the pageant, the eternal ritual of earth.
I return to bed, not to sleep,
But to stay awake wondering
At a power and a wisdom possessed by distant birds,
Who split the night with their cry.

Come Into the Circle of Caring

Come into the circle of caring,
Come into the community of gentleness, of justice and love.
Come, and you shall be refreshed.
Let the healing power of this people penetrate you,
Let loving kindness and joy pass through you,
Let hope infuse you,
And peace by the law of your heart.
In this human circle,
Caring is a calling.
All of us are called.
So come into the circle of caring.

The Pear Trees

There they stand,
two ancient pear trees long past their prime.
They have survived many seasons of ice and snow,
    wind and weather,
though they show their wounds.

Their pears are hard and beyond eating.
They seem to be all bark with no center,
so hollow that one can easily see through them.
Yet life continues to surge through their veins.
Will they burst into bloom again?
Will the leaves come on strong
to hide their worn-out branches?

What keeps them going, year after changing year?
Some ancient hunger for life, no doubt,
a desire to live, to grow and produce.
I cannot yet bring myself to cut them down,
though I fear some strong wind will end them soon.
But who is to know?

And so they stand in silent witness
to the persistence of life.

When Life Is Messy

It is easy to pray when the sun shines
And we are grateful for another glorious day of being.
It is hard to pray when wind and rain and thunder
Plague our every step and spoil our every plan.

It is easy to be virtuous when life goes well
And our existence is a journey from bliss to beauty and back.
It is hard to be virtuous when life assaults us
And our very being is a pilgrimage from bad to worse to
    worst.

It is easy to be cheerful when health bursts in us
So that we can feel the very pulse of life.
It is hard to be happy when pain and fatigue beset us
And we wonder if we can go on.

It is easy to do good when our goodness is rewarded
And we feel the power of pride in accomplishment.
It is hard to do good when we suffer for our efforts
And are troubled because we have been misunderstood.

It is easy to feel religious impulses well up inside us
When inspiration lives at our elbow and walks on our path.
It is hard to feel religious when we are tired with work to be
    done
And discouragement seems to mark our every move.

O God of order and neatness, we give thanks for all that is
good.
We are grateful for manifold blessings bestowed upon us.
O God of chaos and disorder, be with us also when life is
messy.
Bless our coming in and our going out from this day forth.

"Don't Just Do Something, Stand There"

(Inspired by Father Dan Berrigan)

In this holy season of spring we take heart.
The sun rises higher in the sky and the light increases.
The days are longer and warmer now, and we rejoice.
New energy flows in us
And we plunge ourselves into new activity.
It seems as if our spirits have hibernated
And now burst within us as we seek the sun.
Spring is newness, spring is life,
Spring is surging vegetation and the promise of the fall harvest.
It refreshes our spirit and urges us to do more.
But perhaps deep within us there will come an admonition—
Perhaps our frantic busyness will be called into question—
Perhaps we will tap the deeper roots of our spirit.
Don't just do something, it says, stand there.
There is always time to do, to accomplish,
To exert ourselves, to produce food for life.
Don't just do something, stand there. Stand there and notice.
Feel the warmth of the sun on your still back;
Bend down and listen to the sound of growing flowers;
Hear the bird songs that awaken you in the bright morning air;
Pause and smell the blossoms as they race to flower-dom.
Most of all, sense the pulse of life;
Feel the turning of the globe on its still axis,
As it spins to grace us with a truly new season of being.
Feel the earth as it bursts forth with new life—
The tremulous pause before the leap into growth.
Don't just do something, stand there.
Stand there—and be.

Beatitudes for Earth Sunday

Blessed are the heavens,
for they declare the power of creation.
Blessed is the earth, our beloved home,
for she is a planet of plenitude.
Blessed are the waters thereon,
for they gave rise to living things.
Blessed is the land,
for it is the source of life abundant.

Blessed is the air we breathe,
for it fires us to life and love.
Blessed are the beasts of the field,
for they are glorious to behold.
Blessed are the birds of the air,
for they carve a graceful arc in the sky.
Blessed are the mountains and the seas and the valleys,
for their variety makes rich our habitat.

Blessed are the fields of grain, the orchards of fruit,
for they give sustenance, asking nothing in return.
Blessed are the dwellers on earth,
for they cherish the privilege of living upon it.
Blessed are they who protect the earth and all her creatures,
from the plants of the field to the trees of the forest,
for their reward shall be harmony with the web of existence.

Rejoice, and be glad,
for the earth and her people are one.

For Those Who Have Reared Us

(Inspired by "The Invocation to Kali" by May Sarton)

We give thanks for those who have reared us,
Who have nourished us through sleepless nights and restless days,
Who have seen us through the good times and the bad,
Who have celebrated our triumphs
And suffered through our defeats.
We are grateful for their nurturing spirit,
Their gentle touch and their firm hand,
Their familiar laugh and their sympathetic tears.

We acknowledge the unpleasant times as well,
Our struggle to separate ourselves
As children who must make their own way in the world.
We realize our times of ingratitude and selfishness
And resolve to make amends.

We pay silent tribute to the loved ones no longer among us,
And speak soft thanksgiving to those who are.
May we who have been nurtured
Also be nurturers of those who follow;
May we be part of that current of humanity
That courses through time and space.

May we be "gardeners of the spirit"
Even as we have been tended by loving hearts and hands.
On this day may we commingle gratitude
For those who nourished us
And commitment for those
Who receive the gift of life and love from us.
May we be worthy.

What Is Holy?

We sat on the beach transfixed.
The moon not only glimmered across empty space,
But shimmered over a lake now calm
In anticipation of what was to be.

Slowly, timed by some celestial clock,
The curved shadow of earth moved across the lunar surface,
Left to right.
We could not see it move.
All we knew is that inevitably,
As if driven by some chariot-riding god,
It blotted the moon from our sight
Until the glimmering had become only a hinted circle of light,
And the shimmering was swallowed in dark water.

How long we sat there I do not know.
At last, tired in body and mind,
Refreshed in spirit, we silently left for sleep.

"Just another lunar eclipse," the paper said,
"Look again in December."
But there would never be another night like that.
Such moments are not repeated.
It was a holiness that will not fade.

Letting Go Over the Falls

We approached the falls from upstream,
Hearing only a roar designed to intimidate the faint-hearted.
At first glance we saw only white water cascading over the
    cliff
And plunging into the pool in front of us.
The thought that I might be in that water tumbling from an
    unknown height
Kept my heart pounding, adding to the modest exertion of
    the hike.
At last we came into full view:
A lonely mountain river plunging fifteen feet or so,
Swirling through rapids and around rocks to other falls
One definitely would not want to ride.

Stripping to a bathing suit and an old pair of pants—
So as not to rip my one and only swimsuit
And foreshorten my North Carolina swimming career—
I plunged into the lovely pool beneath the falls
To make my way to the point of ascent.
One had to move into the swift current
And then drift to the cable anchored in the rocks.
Clumsily I pulled myself up the rocky slope to the top,
Hand over trembling hand.
Surely, there was no turning back now.
After all, had not my two sons already made the plunge
And lived to tell the tale exuberantly?

I sat in the edge of the stream and nothing happened.
I did not move.
I slowly slid to the center of the stream

But the current did not take me.
I am not certain I wanted to move.
I pushed myself deeper into the stream's center.
Gradually I lost control.

Quickly the current pushed me toward the edge
And even more quickly hurled me over the falls.
I plummeted like a great stone,
Mouth open in a smile of joy or look of terror, I've forgotten
    which,
Down into the deep pool—deeper and deeper.
I could not touch bottom.
Some primordial instinct had me swimming for the air
And I broke the surface water to my own relief
And to the applause of an assembled group
No doubt eager to see if this particular Unitarian Universalist
    divine
Could really walk on water.
Unable (or unwilling) to perform this feat, I swam for the
    rocky shore
To repeat the process with something approaching confident
    joy.

There is something to be said for letting go,
For risking the uncertain,
For putting oneself in strong life currents
With a rich mixture of faith and fear.
Unknown pools sustain us, buoy us;
Forgotten instincts stretch our spirits to the surface
Where the air is clear and the water cold and refreshing.

The Shirk Ethic

O God of Work and Leisure
Teach me to shirk on occasion,
Not only that I may work more effectively
But also that I may enjoy life more abundantly.
Enable me to understand that the earth
Magically continues spinning on its axis
Even when I am not tending thy vineyards.
Permit me to breathe more easily
Knowing the destiny of the race
Rests not on my shoulders alone.
Deliver me from false prophets who urge me
To "repent and shirk no more."
I pray for thy grace on me,
Thy faithful shirker.

Partners in a Cosmic Dance

Consider the cosmos—an eternal dance of mass, energy, and
   spirit.
Consider the stars—how gracefully they wheel through space
In perfect rhythm year by celestial year.
Even obscured by clouds, still they dance,
Their patterns, seen or unseen, engraved in us.
Consider the planets—how they spin and sweep
Always in the same way, never missing a beat,
Their pattern perfect around the mother star,
The intimacy of their dance stored in cosmic knowledge
Beyond our comprehension.

Consider earth which dances and is danced upon.
Faultless is the rhythm of the seasons,
Majestic the axial pivoting which centers the global dance.
Behold the variety of movement—
Spontaneity in the midst of regularity,
Predictable, yet full of surprise.

Consider people and the dance of life—
The initial impulsive movement,
The naive grace that succeeds it,
The rich undulation of maturity,
The deliberate grace of age,
The final rest of death.

We are partners in a cosmic dance.
Let our dancing be for joy.

Embracing the Limits of Life

We gather again in this hallowed place to celebrate life,
To re-create in gratitude our community of faith,
For we have been apart too long.
We come together as different persons than when last we
   met.
Our lives have not stood still—
There are new stories to tell, happy and sad,
As we seek to know one another again.

The happy stories will be easy to relate,
The shared celebration of living will fall quickly from our
   lips.
The sad stories will come with difficulty, sometimes with
   tears,
And we will listen in love to one another.

There are times when life seems without limits—
Boundless, an ever ascending journey, a rising chorus,
A giant crescendo.
We know these are interim times,
For life's inevitabilities crowd upon us.
There is suffering—spiritual and physical—
And there is death—life's last great reminder that we are
   finite.
We are creatures who live within limits.

In the quiet of this hour
May we share our stories,
And as we do so,
May we learn, once again,
To embrace the limits of life.

May we press against those limits
By living and loving to the full,
And learn at last to embrace them
As part of what it is to be alive.

In this hallowed place
And in this holy hour
And with this beloved company,
May we learn to embrace
The limits of life.

The Poignancy of Living in These Days

I inhale and exhale in regular rhythm,
An act so common it never occurs to me to pay attention.
And when I do, I am overwhelmed with the wonder of it all.

I eat my food, as I have done for a thousand thousand days,
A practice so frequent I hardly notice
The miraculous million events that happen in my body.
And when I do, I am taken with their singular beauty.

I greet my loved ones, as I have greeted them for years,
A habit that I pass off casually
Until I realize the deep poignancy of greetings and farewells,
How precious they are,
How they touch deeper feeling chords each time.
Perhaps it is middle age, or old age,
Or perhaps sentiment grows in me,
Or perhaps I am awakening to life
In ways transcending my usual semi-awake state of being.

The poignancy of living in these days
Penetrates me, burrows deep into psyche or soul or spirit—
I know not what.
I only know that I feel things more deeply with the passing
    years,
That the common things of life become uncommon,
That the ordinary becomes extraordinary,
That the habitual becomes sacred.
Bittersweet is the poignancy of living in these days.
I awaken myself,
And bow down in deep gratitude.

Music as Metaphor for Existence

When discussing how he composed his music, Duke Ellington once said that it was good to have limits. He explained that because his trumpet player could reach certain notes beautifully but not other notes, and the same with his trombonist, he had to write his music within those limits.

We live within limits.
We compose a life out of finite time.
We sing the melody of meaning in cathedraled space,
Working out a distinctive tune.
We walk in harmony with all that is,
In cosmos and community,
Seeking to attune ourselves with the music of the spheres,
Knowing our existence is but a single note
In a vast universal symphony.
We move in oscillating rhythms—
Now with bursts of energy,
Now with the richness of repose—
Revelling in the variety of the beat,
Stepping to our own music,
"No matter how measured or far away."
We live within dissonance, for concord is not guaranteed.
Often we are out of tune, inharmonious, out of step.
Dissonance creates its own meaning
Moving within the score,
Providing contrasts that enrich the songs we would sing.
Music is a metaphor for existence.

What We Share

Let us celebrate the common rituals that make us kin:

The poignancy of welcome and farewell,
The anguish of defeat,
The tender touch of those who call us friend;

The exuberant joy of birth,
The empty space in our hearts when a loved one dies,
The ultimate loneliness that each knows,
The warm embrace of comrades who welcome us to the
    celebration of life;

The questions that persist and perplex and do not yield to
    our need for answers,
The shining moments when the sun slants across our dim
    meandering path and illuminates the way,
The strange and anxious excitement of moving on to new
    places to call home;

The fragments of frustration when our best efforts yield
    pitiful results,
The helplessness we feel in a world that sometimes presents
    only problems,
The high joy when some small victory for humanity is won
    and we have helped it happen;

In all our moments of doubt and despair, of problem and
    pain,
Let us remember the common lot shared by our human kin.

In all our times of truth and triumph, of faith and fortitude,
Let us celebrate what we share.
We are, after all, in this together.

In the Holy Quiet of This Hour

In the holy quiet of this hour—
This is sacred time that cannot be taken from us—
These few minutes of calm in an often-hectic week,
This island of serenity in an ocean of events,
This peaceful interlude in the midst of a warring world.

We sit together—a company of believers in life.
If we are still, we can hear a great communal breathing—
The heaving of a hundred chests casting off their burdens,
The inhalation by fellow worshippers who seek the inspiration
Of this time, and of this place, and of this people.
We sense renewal pulsing through our very being;
We sit here to receive the blessings of life—
The memories that drift across our minds,
The hopes harbored in these few moments,
The dreams we dare to conjure in the magic of this time.

Our bodies, tense with the work of the world, relax,
And we know how much we need this time of quietude.
Our minds, burdened with cares and concerns,
Are cleaned and cleared by what we do in this hour.
Our spirits soar with the meaning of this moment—
Above all moments—
This time of being—when there is nothing we must do.

May we take the time,
Here and now,
To celebrate moments like these.
May we savor this intermission from the cares of our lives;
May we be renewed for the living of these days,
And all the days to come.

All this we seek
In the holy quiet of this hour.

Unitarian and Universalist Meditation Manuals

Unitarians and Universalists have been publishing annual editions of prayer collections and meditation manuals for 150 years. In 1841 the Unitarians broke with their tradition of addressing only theological topics and published *Short Prayers for the Morning and Evening of Every Day in the Week, with Occasional Prayers and Thanksgivings*. Over the years, the Unitarians published many volumes of prayers, including Theodore Parker's selections. In 1938 *Gaining a Radiant Faith* by Henry H. Saunderson launched the current tradition of an annual Lenten manual.

Several Universalist collections appeared in the early nineteenth century. A comprehensive *Book of Prayers* was published in 1839, featuring both public and private devotions. During the late 1860s, the Universalist Publishing House was founded to publish denominational materials. Like the Unitarians, the Universalists published Lenten manuals, and in the 1950s they complemented this series with Advent manuals.

Since 1961, the year the Unitarians and the Universalists merged, the Lenten manual has evolved into a meditation manual, reflecting the theological diversity of the two denominations. Today the Unitarian Universalist Association meditation manuals include two styles of collections: poems or short prose pieces written by one author—usually a Unitarian Universalist minister—and anthologies of works by many authors.

The following list includes all meditation manuals since the merger, plus most titles prior to 1961.

Unitarian Universalist

1994   *In the Simple Morning Light* Barbara Rohde‡

1993   *Life Tides* Elizabeth Tarbox‡

       The Gospel of Universalism Tom Owen-Towle‡

1992   *Noisy Stones* Robert R. Walsh‡

1991   *Been in the Storm So Long* Mark Morrison-Reed and
       Jacqui James, Editors‡

1990   *Into the Wilderness* Sara Moores Campbell‡

1989   *A Small Heaven* Jane Ranney Rzepka‡

1988   *The Numbering of Our Days* Anthony Friess Perrino‡

1987   *Exaltation* David B. Parke, Editor‡

1986   *Quest* Kathy Fuson Hurt‡

1985   *The Gift of the Ordinary* Charles S. Stephen, Jr., Editor

1984   *To Meet the Asking Years* Gordon B. McKeeman, Editor

1983   *Tree and Jubilee* Greta W. Crosby

1981   *Outstretched Wings of the Spirit* Donald S. Harrington

1980   *Longing of the Heart* Paul N. Carnes

1979   *Portraits from the Cross* David Rankin

1978   *Songs of Simple Thanksgiving* Kenneth L. Patton

1977   *The Promise of Spring* Clinton Lee Scott

1976   *The Strangeness of This Business* Clarke D. Wells

1975   *In Unbroken Line* Chris Raible, Editor

1974   *Stopping Places* Mary Lou Thompson

1973   *The Tides of Spring* Charles W. Grady

1972   *73 Voices* Chris Raible and Ed Darling, Editors

1971   *Bhakti, Santi, Love, Peace* Jacob Trapp

1970   *Beginning Now* J. Donald Johnston

1969   *Answers in the Wind* Charles W. McGehee

‡ These meditation manuals are available from the Unitarian
Universalist Association. For a free catalog, write to the UUA
Bookstore, 25 Beacon St., Boston, MA 02108-2800.

1968   *The Trying Out* Richard Kellaway

1967   *Moments of Springtime* Rudolf Nemser

1966   *Across the Abyss* Walter D. Kring

1965   *The Sound of Silence* Raymond Baughan

1964   *Impassioned Clay* Ralph Helverson

1963   *Seasons of the Soul* Robert T. Weston

1962   *The Uncarven Image* Phillip Hewett

1961   *Parts and Proportions* Arthur Graham

Council of Liberal Churches (Universalist-Unitarian)

1960   *Imprints of the Divine* Raymond Hopkins

1959   *Indictments and Invitations* Robert B. Cope

1958   *Strange Beauty* Vincent Silliman

1957   *Greatly to Be* Francis Anderson, Jr.

1956   *My Heart Leaps Up* Frank O. Holmes

Unitarian

1955   *The Task Is Peace* Harry Scholefield

1954   *Taking Down the Defenses* Arthur Foote

1953   *My Ample Creed* Palfrey Perkins

1952   *This Man Jesus* Harry C. Meserve

1951   *The Tangent of Eternity* John Wallace Laws

1950   *Deep Sources and Great Becoming* Edwin C. Palmer

1949   *To Take Life Strivingly* Robert Killan

1948   *Come Up Higher* Hurley Begun

1947   *Untitled* Richard Steiner

1946   *The Pattern on the Mountain* (reissue) E. Burdette Backus

1945   *The Expendable Life* Charles G. Girelius

1944   *The Disciplines of Freedom* Leslie T. Pennington

1943   *Faith Forbids Fear* Frederick May Eliot

1942   *Forward into the Light* Frederick W. Griffin

1941   *Victorious Living* W. W. W. Argow

1940   *Address to the Living* Herbert Hitchen

1939   *The Pattern on the Mountain* E. Burdette Backus

1938   *Gaining a Radiant Faith* Henry H. Saunderson

Universalist

1955   *Heritages* Harmon M. Gehr

1954   *Words of Life* Albert F. Ziegler

1953   *Wisdom About Life* Tracy M. Pullman

1952   *Spiritual Embers* John E. Wood

1951   *The Breaking of Bread* Raymond John Baughan

1950   *Add to Your Faith* Roger F. Etz

1949   *To Take Life Strivingly* Robert Killam

1948   *Of One Flame* Robert Cummins

1947   *Using Our Spiritual Resources* Roger F. Etz

1946   *A New Day Dawns* Walter Henry Macpherson

1945   *Beauty for Ashes* Robert and Elsie Barber

1944   *The Price of Freedom* Edson R. Miles

1943   *The Ladder of Excellence* Frank D. Adams

1942   *The Whole Armor of God* Donald B.F. Hoyt

1941   *Earth's Common Things* Max A. Kapp

1940   *The Interpreter* Frederic W. Perkins

1939   *The Great Avowal* Horace Westwood

1938   *Add to Your Faith* Roger F. Etz